Triumph Over Suffering Workbook

A Companion to Triumph Over Suffering

Celeste Li, M.D.

PLUM TREE MINISTRIES

Jupiter, Florida
Requests for information: plumtreeministries@gmail.com
"The surviving remnant of the house of Judah will again take root downward and bear fruit upward." ~ Isaiah 37:31

Triumph Over Suffering Workbook, A Companion to Triumph Over Suffering
Copyright © 2009, 2010, 2015 by Celeste Li
Visit our website at TriumphOverSuffering.com

ISBN-13: 978-0-9841515-9-2
Printed in the United States of America.

All Scripture quotations, unless otherwise indicated, are taken from the Holy Bible: New International Version, NIV, Copyright © 1973, 1978, 1984 by International Bible Society. Used by permission of Zondervan. All rights reserved.
Scripture quotations marked NASB are taken from the New American Standard Bible. Copyright © 1960, 1962, 1963, 1968, 1971, 1972, 1973, 1975, 1977, 1995 by The Lockman Foundation. Used by permission.
Scripture quotations marked NLT are taken from the Holy Bible: New Living Translation, copyright © 1996, 2004. Used by permission of Tyndale House Publishers, Inc., Carol Stream, Illinois 60188. All rights reserved.
Scripture quotations marked KJV are taken from the King James Bible, copyright © 1988 by Liberty University and Thomas Nelson, Inc.

Cover photography and design by Alec Li. Book design and layout by Alec Li.

If you find anything in this book to be valuable for your ministry - whether your ministry is a formal teaching or simply reaching out to your friend - you are welcome to teach it, reprint it, copy it, quote it, or reproduce it in any format, including written, visual, audio, or electronic, without my express permission. If you are quoting other authors whom I have referenced, please give acknowledgment according to industry standards.

To the Plum Tree Ministries Team:
You are dedication personified, and your fervor far exceeds my highest expectations. You have worked with all your heart, as working for the Lord and not for men. A special thank you to my precious friend Donna Briley, who carried this Workbook through to completion. She said "Yes, Lord" to a battle with a giant, and because the battle was the Lord's and her strength was in Him, she defeated the giant with a sling and a stone.

Triumph Over Suffering Workbook

A Companion to Triumph Over Suffering

Infinite Love + Absolute Sovereignty = Intimacy With Christ

Part I: Infinite Love
Experience the Love of God

1	"In This World You Will Have Trouble"	2
2	Experiencing and Expressing Emotions	10
3	Surrender	18

Part II: Absolute Sovereignty
Understand Why We Suffer

4	God Is Sovereign	28
5	Suffering Can Work To Conform Us To the Image of Christ	35
6	Suffering Can Open Our Eyes To Our Sin	42
7	Suffering Can Teach Us Humility, Dependence, and Forgiveness	49
8	Spiritual Warfare: Suffering To Advance the Kingdom	57

Part III: Intimacy With Christ
Seize Your Purpose Through Your Suffering

9	Suffering Can Lead To Intimacy With Christ	66
10	How Will You Respond To Your Suffering?	74
11 & 12	Hearing the Voice of God & Seize What Jesus Seized You For	81

Introduction

If you are hurting, God is reaching down from heaven, for He so desires to touch your heart and spiritually heal you. I am so excited you have chosen to take *Triumph Over Suffering* to a deeper level! God can use this *Workbook* to challenge you, inspire you, convict you, and grow you deeper in Him than you would have ever thought possible. He can use this *Workbook* to destroy the power that suffering has over you. He can use this *Workbook* to penetrate your heart with the keen understanding that living in triumph over adversity does not mean your hardships will be relieved, but that He will give your tribulations great meaning and purpose in Him.

After you read each chapter in the *Triumph Over Suffering* book, grab your pen and open this *Workbook*. You will find each week's lessons will complement the chapter you just read. There is an assignment for each day, including additional Scripture to study and thought-provoking questions to answer. Write your responses to these questions right here in this *Workbook*. The more you pour into this course, the more the Holy Spirit will pour into you. Spiritual growth will not happen without you doing your part: diligently studying His Word with an open heart, and allowing the Holy Spirit to transform you into Christ's image.

The *Triumph Over Suffering* book and this *Workbook* are designed to be used together as a Bible study. You can do this study alone, but your spiritual growth will be enhanced if you have a same gender friend or a group of friends studying and discussing together. Most people find that twelve weeks is a good pace to process the information. If you find you need more time, go ahead and take it at a slower pace; do not put time constraints on the Holy Spirit.

There are seven assignments for each week; each day's assignment will take about a half hour to an hour. You may find some days go more quickly, and some take a little longer. Work to stay on track with a lesson a day; but if your study is interrupted by vacations, children, illness, or every day life, do not let that discourage you. Jump right back in as soon as you can.

Each week has a crucial Scripture verse to memorize after you read each chapter. I encourage you to tuck it away in your heart as one of God's important truths. You may find it helpful to write the verse on an index card to carry around with you for the week, or place it in your car, or hang it up at work or at home.

Most importantly, pray each time before you open your book or workbook, asking the Holy Spirit to be your teacher.

I will be praying for you
as you triumph over suffering.

Part I: Infinite Love
Experience the Love of God

Chapter 1: "In This World You Will Have Trouble"	2
Chapter 2: Experiencing and Expressing Emotions	10
Chapter 3: Surrender	18

Chapter 1
"In This World You Will Have Trouble"

Scripture Verse for the Week:

"In this world you will have trouble. But take heart! I have overcome the world."

John 16:33

Day One: Carefully and contemplatively read Chapter 1, "In This World You Will Have Trouble" in your *Triumph Over Suffering* book. Take it slowly; there is a lot of information to process in each chapter. Re-read parts that are not easy to understand.

You will find each chapter to be packed with Scripture. Which verse speaks to your heart? Write down that verse, and journal your thoughts.

Day Two:

Meditate on this passage from Chapter 1 of your *Triumph Over Suffering* book:

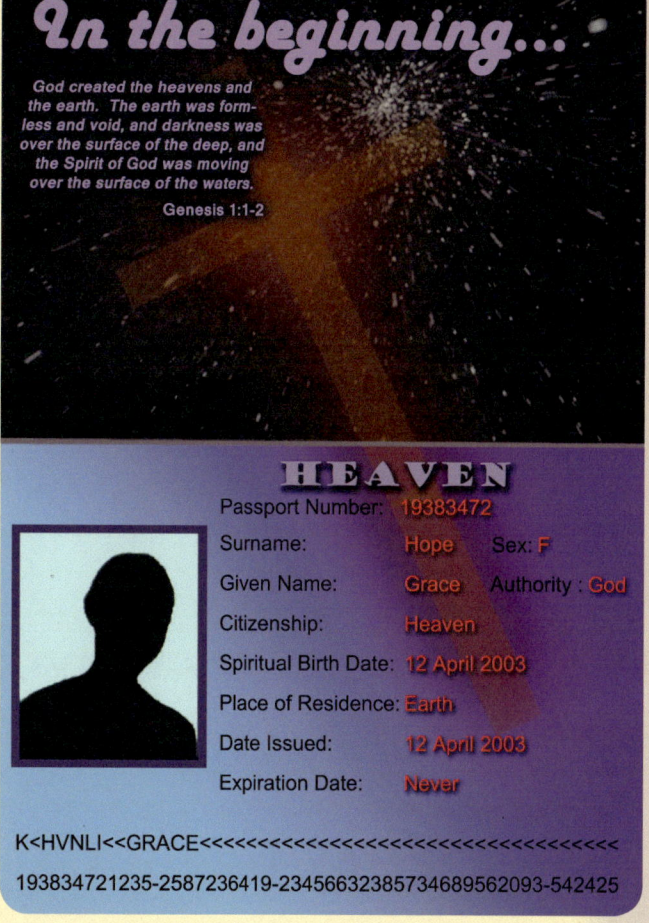

We were not built for this fallen world –
   we were built for eternity.
      (Eccl 3:11)

We do not belong here –
   we are **foreigners and strangers on earth**.
      Hebrews 11:13

We are not citizens here –
   our citizenship is in heaven.
      Philippians 3:20

How does knowing we do not belong here change your perception of this world and your suffering?

Review Elisabeth Kubler-Ross' description of a journey through suffering[1]. Circle the step you are now on, and describe what led you to realize you are here. Is your suffering physical, emotional, spiritual, or a combination?

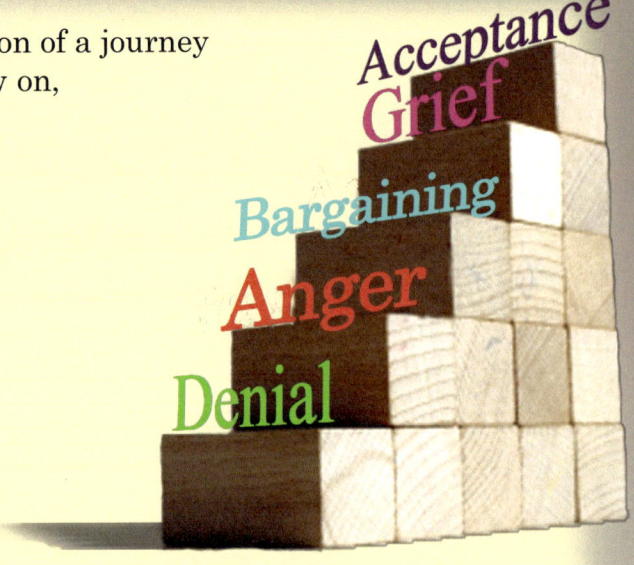

Day Three: The Physical and Mental Disciplines

The Physical Disciplines

Are you taking care of your body as a temple of the Holy Spirit? What will you start doing today to take care of the Holy Spirit's temple?

Read Luke 4:9-12. Have you tested God in the past, or are you testing Him now? What will you start doing today in order to do everything *you* can do and stop testing Him?

---

[1] Elizabeth Kubler-Ross, *On Death and Dying*, New York, NY, Scribner, 1969, p 9.

The Mental Disciplines

Go over the mental disciplines in your *Triumph Over Suffering* book. Which of these are your strong points? Which ones will you focus on strengthening? How?

Change your response to suffering

Connect with Christian friends

Help others

Journal

Read how God commanded some of His people to journal in Exodus 17:14, Jeremiah 30:2, and Habakkuk 2:2. There are several types of spiritual journaling you can do:

- Working through a Bible study journal, such as this one you have in your hands right now.
- Pouring out your innermost emotions and desires and pains to God.
- Journaling by reading daily Scripture, and writing what God is saying to you through those passages and how you will apply it to your life.
- Journaling experiences with God and how He has moved in your life.

Buy a simple notebook and commit to keeping a journal today.

Day Four: : Ask the Holy Spirit to reveal to you how your spiritual three-legged stool looks. Circle the stool that represents you, and write on the legs: Bible, Prayer, and Church. If you have more than one leg damaged, and your stool is even more unstable than the one pictured here, draw your own broken stool.

If your stool is not stable, what will you do to repair the broken legs?

Bible: 2 Timothy 3:16 states the bible is useful for four reasons. How are these reasons different? How are they related?

When we immerse in His Word, and God grows us in this way, the end result is verse 17. Can you see why Scripture study is paramount?

Read Psalm 119:11. What is the outcome of Scripture study and memorization?

Look up Hebrews 4:12. What do you think "living and active" means? What do you think "divide soul and spirit, joints and marrow" means?

Write down your commitment to start reading your Bible every day. Include where in the Bible you will start, and what place and time of day you will read.

By the end of this course, this will be an ingrained spiritual discipline that you will not stop. As you grow in Him, you will develop a hunger to spend more time alone with Him. Spend today's time alone with God right now.

Day Five: *Prayer*

I love the Lord because he hears and answers my prayers. Because he bends down and listens I will pray as long as I have breath!
Psalm 116:1-2 NLT

He bends down and listens . . . our prayers are so precious to Him. Does that not make you want to pray right now? Journal your thoughts here.

Is there an order of prayer? Yes, and no. First realize that prayer is not to be done in an obsessive sort of way. When we are praying without ceasing, we are simply talking to Him and listening for His guidance. Also, there will often be times when we simply cry out to God to rescue us because of the desperateness of the situation.

Nevertheless, Jesus did teach His disciples not to burst into the throne room demanding or petitioning, but to remember to whom they are speaking! It is crucial we set aside time at least once a day to be still before God, and it is for these times that Jesus taught His disciples the order of prayer that pleases our heavenly Father. Read Matthew 6:9-13. Jesus' intent was not for His disciples to repeat the "Our Father" prayer word-for-word (Mt 6:7). These verses are a model Jesus gave His disciples to follow, what to pray for and in what order. Read this passage and write down in your own words what our Father desires us to address in prayer and in what order.

Day Six: *Prayer*

Write down two things that can hinder your prayers. (Refer to Chapter 1 in your *Triumph Over Suffering* book in the section entitled *Second Leg: Prayer*.)

1- _____

2- _____

Read the following verses and list additional hindrances to prayer.

Matthew 5:23-24: _____

Psalm 100:4: _____

Psalm 46:10a: _____

James 1:5: _____

Matthew 6:10: _____

Are any of these hindering your prayers? What will you do to break through the barrier?

Day Seven: *Your Church Family*

The church, all believers, are the body of Christ (Eph 1:23). *The Purpose Driven Life* explains that as members of God's church, we have privileges, yet also five responsibilities, or purposes[1]. Look up the Scripture references and write down each of the five purposes in the points of the star.

Around the star: Psalm 34:3, Hebrews 10:25, Colossians 1:7, 1 Peter 4:10, 2 Cor 5:18-20

Because of your suffering, you may feel unable to fulfill each one of these purposes. The goal of this course is to guide you to understand God's purposes for you through your suffering. As you immerse yourself in this study, God will pour into you His love and comfort, and the Holy Spirit will grow you spiritually so that you will be ready to fulfill all of these purposes.

Pray and journal, evaluating whether or not you are fulfilling these purposes. Determine what you will change. As you consider the first purpose, glorifying God through worship, realize that going to the beach or walking in the woods can be special time alone in prayer with God, appreciating His creation and closing out the noises and busyness of the world. Yet the Spirit comes down in a unique way when believers are gathered together to worship (Mt 18:20).

Stick with this Workbook *and God will reward you for persevering. Scripture study is a key component of the spiritual growth of this course. When we read His living and active Word with an open heart, we will not leave His Presence unchanged. God's Word will divide soul and spirit as we are convicted of sin, and God reveals our beliefs and attitudes that do not line up with His thoughts.*

---

[1] Rick Warren, *The Purpose Driven Life*, Grand Rapids, MI, Zondervan, 2002, p320-322.

Chapter 2
Experiencing and Expressing Emotions

Scripture Verse for the Week:

Search me, O God, and know my heart;
Test me and know my anxious thoughts.
See if there is any offensive way in me,
And lead me in the way everlasting.

Psalm 139:23-24

Day One: Read Chapter 2, Experiencing and Expressing Emotions, in your *Triumph Over Suffering* book. Go into this chapter trusting Jesus to hold your hand as you open yourself up to experience emotions you may not even know you have.

Which verse speaks to your heart? Write down that verse, and journal your thoughts.

Day Two: Why all the focus on emotions? We cannot crush our undesirable emotions without crushing the desirable emotions. It is natural for us as humans not to want to examine ourselves. None of us likes to admit our shortcomings and sins. Yet we choose to do this because we know that it is the only way to grow closer to God. It is sin that keeps us estranged from God, and our repentance and His forgiveness that draws us near.

Fill in the factors of your upbringing, education, and experiences that you see are critical factors affecting the way you handle emotions today. Circle the factors that you perceive have the greatest influence.

Upbringing	Education	Experience

How would you rate your ability to handle emotions? Are your emotions stunted? Raging out of control? Do you control your emotions, or do your emotions control you? Pray, and journal what God shows you.

In Chapter 2 in your *Triumph Over Suffering* book, go over the section entitled *Handling Emotions*. What will you apply to your life right now?

Day Three: *Anger*

God called Jonah to preach repentance to the Ninevites. Jonah ran away, was swallowed by the great fish, vomited up and sent to Nineveh. Read Jonah's response to Nineveh's repentance (Jonah 3:10 – 4:11). Is this sinful anger? Why?

What is God's response to Jonah's anger? (see Jonah 4:4)

Let's move to Job. Job was blameless and upright (Job 1:1), yet he suffered much, because God gave Satan permission to attack him (Job 1:12). Read Job Chapter 3.
Job spends the next 34 chapters ruled by uncontrolled anger, full of frustration, bitterness, and hatred. Can you relate? Journal your thoughts.

Read a portion of God's answer to Job's questions, Job 38:1-7. Not much of an explanation to Job for why he suffered . . . or is it? What do you think?

Read Job 42:6, the blameless and upright man's response to God's answer. What do you think of his response?

Day Four: *Anger*

God pointed out to Jonah and Job that their anger had crossed the line into sin. It seems God gave them time to try to figure that out for themselves. When they did not, when they were consumed with bitterness, hatred, and revenge, He pointed out the error of their ways. He then gave them a chance to repent and return to a loving relationship with Him. What insights does this give you about how God treats His loved ones?

Are you angry? Is your anger a feeling that you are allowing to wash over you and pass on, or is it destroying you? Anger is sinful when it leads to resentment, bitterness, hatred, or revenge. With God's help, determine if you are in sinful anger. Write a prayer of repentance, and request His power to overcome this sin and move out of this emotional turmoil.

Write in your own words the difference between righteous and unrighteous anger. (Refer to Chapter 2 in your *Triumph Over Suffering* book, the section entitled *Righteous Anger vs. Unighteous Anger*.) Is your anger righteous or unrighteous? Why?

Day Five: Self-Pity and Guilt

Self-Pity

Is it easier to be a victim than a hero? Do you like the attention? Is your disease a reason to avoid some responsibilities? Are your tribulations an excuse not to live up to God's expectations?

Self pity can be difficult to root out. For some of us, there may be some pleasure in it. We may like the relief this excuse brings. Yet dig deeper inside and admit that there is no true fulfillment in living this lie. It is a thief, sent to rob us of hope and purpose.

self-pity = selfishness

Journal your thoughts. If you are in self-pity, write a prayer to the Lord to request His help in finding true joy and contentment as you fulfill His purpose for you in this life.

Guilt

Write in your own words the difference between the types of guilt. (Refer to Chapter 2 in your *Triumph Over Suffering* book in the section *Guilt*.)

1- Godly Sorrow (true guilt)

2- Two Types of Worldly Sorrow (false guilt)

      1-

      2-

Are you living with guilt? Ask the Holy Spirit to speak to you as you fill in the chart below as it applies to your life.

True Guilt	False Guilt: Pretended Guilt	False Guilt: Imposed by the world, others, self

How does your Itty Bitty Should-Have Committee berate you? Fill in the bubbles.

What will you do to eliminate your Itty Bitty Should-Have Committee?

Day Six: *Depression* - Go over the subtle looks of depression and the keys to overcoming it detailed in the book under the section *Depression*. Are you depressed? Which of these keys are you missing? Pray, and journal what God reveals to you.

Worry and Anxiety

Write in your own words the difference between the world's peace and God's peace. Do you think if you had God's peace the circumstances of the world would be able to shake that profound spiritual peace?

The fruit of righteousness will be peace; the effect of righteousness will be quietness and confidence forever. Isaiah 32:17

Righteous means we are in right standing with God. Realize that only Jesus' death and resurrection make us truly righteous. When we surrender to Jesus as our Lord and Savior, He comes to live inside of us and infuses His righteousness into us (2 Cor 5:21). Yet we are also commanded to live a righteous life, in obedience to God's will and His ways. This does not mean that we are sinless or perfect, but that when we sin, we repent, ask His forgiveness, and seek to conform our life to His holy standards (Mt 5:48).

We will fail to experience God's peace when we are sinning and not repentant. Ask God to reveal to you any areas where you may not be living righteously. What will you do now?

Day Seven: *Fear*

What or whom do you fear? Do you have a spirit of fear?

Go over three tools to defeat fear in your *Triumph Over Suffering* book in the section entitled *Fear*. Which one is most valuable for you? How will you utilize it?

1 Peter instructs us to cast all our anxiety on Him (1 Pet 5:7). Understand that casting your anxiety on Him will not make your problems disappear. It only means that your problems will no longer be master over you, they will no longer be able to produce anxiety, worry, or fear. Why do you think God commands us to fling, to heave, to hurl our anxieties upon Him?

You did a lot of work already! The first two chapters form the base necessary to process the rest of this course. Take some time now alone with God and honestly evaluate your level of deep inner peace. If you are not at peace, could it be because you have not completely surrendered your life to God?

Chapter 3
Surrender

Scripture Verse for the Week: As you memorize this verse, think deeply about what price was paid and who paid it.

You are not your own; you were bought at a price.
1 Corinthians 6:19-20

Day One: Read Chapter 3, Surrender, in your *Triumph Over Suffering* book.

If, through Chapter 3, you have not made a choice to surrender, that is okay. You cannot rush it or force yourself, and no one can talk you into it. This is a very serious personal decision just between you and God. For some specific encouragement and assignments, skip to page 25 in this *Workbook* to the section entitled *If You Have Not Made a Choice To Surrender*.

If you have recently surrendered to Jesus, or are already living a life of deep surrender to Him, do proceed with this week's journaling. Becoming more sensitive to His Spirit is important for all of us.

If, through Chapter 3, you have just made a choice to surrender, either a first-time surrender or coming into a deeper surrender to Jesus, brace yourself, for you are right now going through some amazing experiences! Go ahead and journal right here the intense passion of your encounter with your Creator.

If your surrender came with any commitments, write them down so you will hold yourself accountable and will not forget.

Day Two: Surrender often gives us . . .

- An incredible urge to pray and worship God, and an intense connection to Him like you have never experienced before. Bask in it!
- A great hunger for God's Word, and a supernatural ability to understand it. Allow God to teach you not by commentaries, but by His own Spirit.
- A burning desire to connect with other believers who have come into a deep surrender themselves. Be sure you are sharing with your spouse or with a same gender friend. Do not become entangled in an emotional relationship to discuss "spiritual" things with someone of the opposite gender. This type of deep sharing is to be reserved for your spouse or a friend of the same gender.

Journal your experiences.

Surrender often opens our eyes to sins we were ignoring. This is a very crucial time. Do not quench the Holy Spirit; repent and make restitution immediately, no matter how difficult or humbling it is. Turn 180 degrees away from your sin. Apologize to those you have hurt. Make up for wrongs you have done as best you are able. The more you obey God in your repentance, the closer you will grow to Him. Spend time today still before God asking Him to reveal your sin to you, and journal what He shows you.

Day Three: When you surrender your life to Christ for the first time, the Holy Spirit comes to live inside you. When you enter into a deeper surrender, you receive a fresh filling of the Holy Spirit as you surrender more of your heart to His control. We will explore some areas where you may now recognize the Spirit working in your life and heart. Do not be discouraged if you do not sense God moving; these exercises are simply to train your spirit to be sensitive to His Spirit.

Some people say that when they surrender, they feel as if a great weight has been lifted off them. This is a twofold weight: the weight of sin lifted off you as your receive His forgiveness, and the weight of problems that you have given to Jesus. Write the sins and problems that you have released to Jesus on the buckets. Add more lines if needed.

How does it feel to have Jesus lift this burden from you?

Read Matthew 11:28-30. Notice that when we give Jesus our burdens, we are now yoked to Him. We have work to do – with a glorious Partner! What do you think that work entails?

Day Four: You may find you are on fire to tell people what Jesus has done in your life. Do it! When you have just made this decision, when you are flush with excitement and pure praise of God, you are a powerful testimony to others. Tell everyone you can. Read Mark 5:1-20. Note what Jesus instructed the man to do in verse 19, and what he did.

Make a list below of everyone you will tell about your decision for Christ, especially your family and close friends, and start telling them today!

A word of caution: As much as you would like those you love to surrender to Jesus right now, remember you cannot rush people, force them into it, or talk them into it. This is a personal decision between a person and God. It is easy to become angry or frustrated with those who are refusing Christ. Maintain the heart of Christ and love them no matter where they are spiritually. It may be the testimony of your changed life, which they observe gradually, which is the greatest influence you can have on them. Remember, we can be God's instruments, but *only Jesus saves*.

Day Five: One of the most treasured results of surrender is that God reveals to us His purpose for us, the purpose for which He designed us. For some, this comes as a huge calling all at once; for others, it is a more gradual understanding of God's plan for them, like a far distant object that at first is blurry but then comes into focus as we get closer. This is another area where it is crucial not to quench the Holy Spirit. Do not be frightened by the enormity of God's call, for God will **equip you with everything good for doing his will (**Heb 13:21).

Pray for a purpose, a vision, God's plan for your life, and journal what He shows you. Do not be discouraged if you hear nothing. In upcoming chapters you will learn about hearing the voice of God and allowing God to reveal His purpose for you.

If God has given you a calling, e-mail me at CJL@TriumphOverSuffering.com so I can encourage you and lift you up in prayer. If you are waiting on His perfect timing for a calling, e-mail me so we can spur one another on toward love and good deeds.

Day Six: Read Psalm 139:1-10, and feel God's powerful love for you. He knows you, so deeply, even more than you know yourself.

Continue reading Psalm 139:13-16. Look at the cover of this book, noting the Potter's scars that speak of His infinite love. Picture the Potter so painstakingly molding you. He is magnificent in His ingenuity, creating each person so uniquely, to fit perfectly into His Kingdom plan. How much He must cherish *you*, for you are His treasured handiwork. "God does not make junk." What parts of your body or your life do you wish were different?

If I settle on the far side of the sea, even there your hand will guide me, your right hand will hold me fast. —Psalm 139:9-10

Meditate on this psalm, and allow God to change *your* perspective to *His* perspective. Then journal your new outlook on your life and suffering.

Continue reading Psalm 139:17-18. God's thoughts of us: countless. Pause for a moment to take all of that in.

Day Seven:

The Lord your God is with you, he is mighty to save. He will take great delight in you, he will quiet you with his love, he will rejoice over you with singing.

Zephaniah 3:17

Did you know God sings? Sings as He rejoices over us? What do you think His singing sounds like? Let your imagination run wild as you meditate on this verse and write a prayer to our singing God.

Read Romans 8:32 and 35-39. Jesus came from the everlasting to die a death of crucifixion *for you*. Is there anything good He will hold back from you? Think about your trials, pains, tribulations, and hardships. They cannot separate you from His love, but you can allow this pain to create a barrier that will thwart your experience of His love. Have you erected a barrier? What will you do to break through that barrier?

Move to Part II, Absolute Sovereignty. You are now ready for the very challenging Scriptures in Chapter 4. Cling tightly to Jesus, and He will grow your roots deep and cause you to bear much fruit.

If You Have Not Made a Choice to Surrender

Surrender is profoundly personal and is just between you and God. Spend your time this week meditating on God's love for you, and evaluating your decision not to surrender. This is a very heavy, very difficult decision that cannot be taken lightly. It took me many months to come to that decision! It is also a decision that you cannot fake, for God knows your heart. A superficial surrender is no surrender at all.

Do not give up on this study! There is much God wants to teach you through this course. If you are not ready now to choose for Christ, it is possible you may be ready in a few weeks. Here are some suggestions that may help you in your decision:

- Carefully, prayerfully, out loud or in a whisper, review the Scripture from Chapter 3, Surrender, in your *Triumph Over Suffering* book.

- You may find helpful these two links on the Triumph Over Suffering web site, http://www.triumphoversuffering.com: *Do You Know Jesus?* and *Surrender*.

- If you are not reading your Bible, start today. This is the most important key to drawing you closer to God and helping you in your decision. Start in the beginning of the New Testament. If you are already reading your Bible, don't give up! For me, it took many months of daily Bible reading to comprehend surrender, and then many more months before I was ready to choose Christ.

- If you truly want to surrender, but feel you are not quite ready, or something is holding you back, pray, asking God to bring you to that decision for Christ.

- If you know a deeply surrendered Christian, your spouse or a same gender friend, someone who has a strong and growing relationship with Jesus, it may help to talk to them. Ask them how they came to their decision to surrender, and how their lives have changed now that they are living for Jesus.

- Work through Days 6 and 7 in this chapter of this *Workbook*. Then we will study Psalm 91 together on the next page.

Read Psalm 91:1-16. (When you read in the Old Testament about enemies, you can understand those enemies to mean Satan and his demons.)

> **He who dwells in the shelter of the Most High**
> **Will rest in the shadow of the Almighty.**
>
> Psalm 91:1

God Most High is El Elyon, a Name of God that describes God as "Sovereign Ruler of the Universe,"[1] controlling everything in heaven and on earth.

Almighty is El Shaddai, a Name of God that means "The All-Sufficient One."[2] This Name "describes power, but not of violence, but of bountifulness."[3] It means that God is all-powerful and pours forth His blessings upon us; all that we have, all that we are, and all that we need comes from Him.

So what does this verse mean? When we acknowledge God as El Elyon, Sovereign God in control of all the universe, and surrender *completely* to Him and trust Him fully, then we will be at peace, resting in El Shaddai's shadow, knowing that God Almighty will protect us and care for us and meet all our needs.

If you are not at peace, could it be that you have not acknowledged God as El Elyon, Sovereign God in control of your entire life? Could it be because you have not completely surrendered to Him, given Him complete control of your life? Journal your thoughts.

Please e-mail me at CJL@TriumphOverSuffering.com so I can support you, pray for you, and answer any questions you may have.

---

[1] Kay Arthur, *Lord, I Want to Know You*, Colorado Springs, CO, Waterbook Press, 2000, p 15.
[2] Arthur, p 37.
[3] Andres Jukes, *The Names of God*, Grand Rapids, MI, Kregel Publications, 1976, p 74.

Part II: Absolute Sovereignty

Understand Why We Suffer

4	God Is Sovereign	28
5	Suffering Can Work To Conform Us To the Image of Christ	35
6	Suffering Can Open Our Eyes To Our Sin	42
7	Suffering Can Teach Us Humility, Dependence, and Forgiveness	49
8	Spiritual Warfare: Suffering To Advance the Kingdom	57

Chapter 4
God Is Sovereign

Scripture Verse for the Week:

The Lord Almighty has sworn, "Surely, as I have planned, so it will be, and as I have purposed, so it will stand..." For the Lord Almighty has purposed, and who can thwart him? His hand is stretched out, and who can turn it back?

Isaiah 14:24,27

Day One: Before you read this chapter, take a moment to come quietly into God's presence, allowing His love to pour into your heart. Now, with a heart wide open to the Holy Spirit's teaching, read Chapter 4, God Is Sovereign, in your *Triumph Over Suffering* book.

Which verse speaks to your heart? Write down that verse, and journal your thoughts.

Day Two: This chapter was extremely challenging, yet crucial in grasping an understanding of suffering. Whether you will comprehend the rest of this course hinges on whether you will accept God's absolute sovereignty. Spend some time in prayer, allowing God to illuminate your beliefs hidden deep in your heart. When God has revealed to you your level of acceptance of His sovereignty, draw a figure of yourself standing on the graph.

Are you satisfied with your level of acceptance of this critical attribute of God? Is God satisfied? If not, what will you do to move up on the graph?

Resisting **Developing** **Accepting**

Read John 8:31-32 to find out how we can come to know the truth of who God is, of what His sovereignty means. Note that the word *disciple* means "more ... than a mere pupil or learner. It is an adherent who accepts the instruction given to him and makes it his rule of conduct."[1] Write down what you have learned from today's study, and what it will mean for you to truly live as His disciple.

---

[1] Spiros Zodhiates, *The Complete Word Study Dictionary New Testament*, Chattanooga, TN, AMC Publishers, 1992, p 936 (no. 3101).

Day Three: It is imperative that you understand that when God ordains suffering for you, He does not let Satan run rampant through your life. You read in your *Triumph Over Suffering* book this week that God had placed a hedge of protection around Job. Satan had to ask permission to touch Job and was only given limited powers. Read Luke 22:24-34 and 54-62 to see again how Satan must ask permission and is only granted limited access.

Why do you think God gave Satan permission to sift Peter like wheat? (Hint: What were the disciples discussing in verse 24? Who do you think the disciples considered the greatest?)

Study the reasons listed why God allows suffering in the section entitled *Bottom of the Tapestry* in Chapter 4 of your *Triumph Over Suffering* book. Which of these reasons do you think applies to Peter's situation?

Do you think any of these apply to your situation? Open your heart to the Holy Spirit, and journal what He reveals to you.

Day Four: Before studying this chapter, did you feel like the person pictured here? Do you still feel this way?

Explain in your own words how God steers evil to accomplish His purposes without violating free will. Refer to *Are We Puppets?* and H*ow Can God Have Sovereignty and We have Free Will?* in your *Triumph Over Suffering* book if needed.

In your *Triumph Over Suffering* book, read over the verses from Acts in *Are We Puppets?* and the definition of decree in the next section. Can you accept that the Trinity ordained Jesus' death, willed it, determined it, decreed it, planned it before the universe was even created? What do you think of a God who creates a world while knowing that He will be brutally murdered to redeem the people He creates?

Day Five: Do you ever ask, "Why me?" Go ahead and honestly journal.

Read Job Chapters 38 - 41. These chapters are God's answer to Job's question of "Why me?" They are very humbling chapters. Write your comments on what God is saying in these chapters.

Day Six: Faith is trusting God when we only see the bottom of the tapestry. We *will* see the Master Craftsman's beautiful workmanship on the top of the tapestry someday, even if we must wait until eternity to view it. But in the meantime, in the here and now, we may only see the bottom side.

Fill in the chart below. On the left side, list times in your life when you only saw the bottom of the tapestry. On the right side, describe when God later gave you a glimpse of the top. You may have a lot more to write on the left side than on the right! Save this journal, and fill in the right side over the next weeks, months, or even years as God reveals His work on the top of the tapestry.

Bottom of the Tapestry	Glimpse of the Top

Day Seven: Read 1 Timothy 5:24.

We must understand that justice is not completed on earth. Some sins are revealed before death and given earthly punishment; some are not revealed until after death. But at the end of the world, every mouth will be silenced because God's justice will be so fair that none will be able to complain (Rom 3:19).

Read Psalm 73. Have you ever felt this way? Envious of the arrogant and wicked who seem to have no struggles? Do you wonder if God even notices (verse 11)?

What caused the psalmist to change his heart? (Hint: verse 17). What does it mean to go into God's sanctuary?

In verses 21 and 22, what does the psalmist say he was like before he came humbly before God for understanding? In verse 24, what does coming humbly into God's sanctuary accomplish in the psalmist? How can you apply this to your life right now?

You have completed a very weighty chapter, and I pray you have encountered the Living God as never before. As you peer up at the bottom of the tapestry, remember not to separate His infinite love from His absolute sovereignty.

Chapter 5
Suffering Can Work To Conform Us
To the Image of Christ

Scripture Verse for the Week:

And we know that God causes all things to work together for good to those who love God, to those who are called according to His purpose. For those whom He foreknew, He also predestined to become conformed to the image of His Son.

Rom 8:28-29 NASB

Day One: Before reading today, take a moment to drink in the cover of the book again. Allow your eyes to rest on the Potter's nail-scarred hands that speak of the depth of His love for you. Then read Chapter 5, Suffering Can Work To Conform Us To the Image of Christ, in your *Triumph Over Suffering* book.

Which verse speaks to your heart? Write down that verse, and journal your thoughts.

Day Two: Only the Potter knows our purpose, because He created us. If we are fighting against His molding and shaping of us, because we are trying to be that vase and He has ordained for us to be a bowl, He may need to take us through a lot to configure us for His purposes. Yet if we are flexible for Him, we will more smoothly be molded by His touch. Are you fighting the Potter, or are you soft putty in His hands?

What if He never has planned for you to be a vase? What if you are called to be a bowl? Can you accept that?

"Sharp fragments of broken pottery," or potsherds were used in Jesus' time only in menial ways, "to scoop burning coals from a fire or to scrape boils."[1] I have heard that potsherds were also used for "scrap paper." Read about us potsherds in Isaiah 45:9-12.

Jesus died for us potsherds! Do not miss the fervor of His love. Just do not forget that He is in charge. Nothing spectacular and nothing painful enters your life without God ordaining it. Before He created the universe, He crafted your every moment. Absolute sovereignty + infinite love. Journal your thoughts.

[2] Warren Baker and Eugene Carpenter, *The Complete Word Study Dictionary Old Testament*, Chattanooga, TN, AMG Publishers, 2003, p 383 (no. 2789).

Day Three:

> [20] But who are you, O man, to talk back to God? "Shall what is formed say to him who formed it, 'Why did you make me like this?' " [21] Does not the potter have the right to make out of the same lump of clay some pottery for noble purposes and some for common use?
>
> [22] What if God, choosing to show his wrath and make his power known, bore with great patience the objects of his wrath--prepared for destruction? [23] What if he did this to make the riches of his glory known to the objects of his mercy, whom he prepared in advance for glory-- [24] even us, whom he also called, not only from the Jews but also from the Gentiles?
>
> Romans 9:20-24

This is an extremely challenging passage that can be interpreted on different levels; I certainly do not understand all the nuances of these verses. I think that one of the keys in understanding these verses is the word **prepared**. The word and tense for **prepared in advance** in verse 23 mean "to prepare beforehand ... to appoint before."[1] *God* prepared these people, equipped them in advance, for glory. The people being prepared for glory are those who belong to Jesus, the objects of His mercy. Do not forget that God offers His mercy to everyone (Jn 3:16-17); each of us chooses whether we want to accept it or not, whether we want to be objects of His mercy, whether we want Him to prepare us in advance for glory.

Prepared[3,4] in verse 22 (**prepared for destruction**) is a completely different word and tense in the Greek. It means that *they* "fitted *themselves* unto destruction. They were *not* fitted for destruction by God."[2] These people *chose* destruction themselves. It was their free will.

What if God allows those who are rejecting Him, who are preparing themselves for an eternity without God, to continue on this earth, wreaking suffering on us, the objects of His mercy, in order to reveal His glory in us? Staggering! I can hardly wrap my mind around this. Your turn to journal now.

---

[1] Zodhiates, p 1219 (no. 4282).
[2] Zodhiates, p 843 (no. 2675), emphasis mine.

Day Four:

We are going to tackle one more section today to grasp a further understanding of how God has sovereignty *and* we have free will. Read Romans 9:14-18.

Romans 9:16 tells us **it does not depend on man's desire or effort, but on God's mercy.** His mercy. Not His wrath, or His judgment, but His *mercy*.

The example used here for an object of wrath who prepared himself for destruction is Pharaoh. Romans 9:17 teaches us that God raised Pharaoh up, placed him in a position of power, so that through Him God will be glorified. The Israelites' dramatic and almost unbelievable escape from slavery under Pharaoh would not have given God nearly so much glory if Pharaoh had not been such a mighty and seemingly invincible king.

Read these verses and write after each verse who hardened Pharaoh's heart:
  Exodus 8:15 (after the plague of frogs lifted): _____
  Exodus 8:32 (this occurs a few plagues later): _____
  Exodus 9:12 (this occurs a few plagues later): _____

Note that first Pharaoh repeatedly hardened his *own* heart, and *then* God hardened his heart. Pharaoh came to a point of no return. Spend some time in prayer and journaling.

Day Five: **It is God's will that you should be sanctified.** 1 Thessalonians 4:3

Sanctified is "to be set apart from a common to a sacred use." It describes "separation, consecration, devotion to the service of Deity, sharing in God's purity and abstaining from earth"s defilement."[1] After we surrender our lives to Jesus, we embark on a lifetime of sanctification, being conformed to Christ's image. In heaven, God will glorify us and take the sanctification process to completion. So why bother with all the sanctification here? Do you think it has anything to do with your Kingdom work here on earth?

Will is thelema; my Word Study says it is "not to be conceived as a demand, but as an expression or inclination of pleasure."[2] When we are sanctified, we give Him delight. Astounding! Can you imagine giving the Creator of the Universe *delight*? Write a prayer to God.

Read Jesus' parable about the Kingdom of Heaven in Matthew 25:14-28. God is preparing useful, rewarding, satisfying work for us in heaven! Realize our sanctification on earth is preparing us for heavenly rewards – and also heavenly *responsibilities*. Does that make you look at your sanctification in a whole new light?

---
[1] Zodhiates, p 70 (no. 40).
[2] Zodhiates, p 721 (no. 2307).

Day Six: In 2 Corinthians 4, Paul is writing about suffering and tribulation. Read 2 Corinthians 4:16-18 and write it here:

When we are suffering, what is happening externally? _____

What is happening to us internally? _____

Paul has been persecuted, beaten, imprisoned, yet he calls these troubles **light and momentary**! Why do you think he uses these words? Do you think he is being sarcastic, or do you think he is comparing them to something else, so in comparison they really do appear light and momentary?

What is their suffering achieving for them? _____

Paul is able to speak this way about his sufferings because he is fixing his

eyes on _____

For what is seen, the suffering, is _____

But what is unseen, our glory, is _____

This is a critical verse to have tucked in your heart.

Day Seven:

He will sit as a refiner and purifier of silver. Malachi 3:3

A silversmith explained that in refining silver, he must hold the silver in the middle of the fire where the flames are hottest so as to burn away all the impurities. He must sit there in front of the fire the whole time the silver is being refined in order to keep his eyes on the silver, for if the silver is left even a moment too long in the flames, it will be destroyed.

How does he know when the silver is fully refined? When he sees his image reflected in it.[1]

Stunning. God is the Silversmith, holding us in the fire to refine us, purify us, remove all the unwanted material. He must keep His eye on us at every moment so we will not be destroyed. And we will not be finished with the purification process until we reflect His image. You must have much to journal now!

Take a moment to study the cover of this book again, noting the nail wounds in the Potter. Keep this image of His love in your mind each time you find yourself sitting on the Potter's wheel, or in the Refiner's fire.

---
[1] Unknown Author; Distributed out at the 2005 Ladies Retreat at the Valley Church of Christ, Wasilla, AK.

Chapter 6
Suffering Can Open Our Eyes To Our Sin

Scripture Verse for the Week:

"My son, do not regard lightly the discipline of the Lord, nor faint when you are reproved by Him; for those whom the Lord loves He disciplines, and He scourges every son whom He receives." . . . He disciplines us for our good, so that we may share His holiness.

Hebrews 12:5-6, 10 NASB

Day One: Read Chapter 6, Suffering Can Open Our Eyes To Our Sin, in your *Triumph Over Suffering* book. This is a very convicting chapter. Do not quench the Holy Spirit, but allow Him to speak to your heart. Before you read, decide right now to act on whatever He tells you.

You may not want to allow God access into the darkest corners of your heart. But stick with your *Workbook* this week, for when you are purified a little more and a little more, the joy and peaceful fruit of righteousness you receive will far outweigh the pain of the purification.

Which verse speaks to your heart? Write down that verse, and journal your thoughts.

Chapter 6 ~ *Suffering Opens Our Eyes To Our Sin*   43

Day Two: Yesterday you read in Revelation that we were created for God's pleasure. That humbles me to the dust. Journal your thoughts.

Fill in the diagram depicting a time when you multiplied the intensity of your suffering by your own sinful choices. Write the initial trial or suffering in the boulder on the left. Write on the arrows your poor choices that multiplied your suffering. Describe the greater suffering in the boulder on the right. Add more arrows if you need them.

Look up Psalm 32:9. Describe a time when you were like a mule needing a bit to draw near to God. Do you ever want to be *that* rebellious again?

Day Three: Go over your memory verses for this week again. These are very difficult verses! What do you think of God scourging us to bring us to repentance? Describe a time in your life when you were scourged in this way. Is it worth it . . . to share His holiness?

Disciplining us and opening our eyes to our sin are not punishments. The difference between discipline and punishment is the heart attitude of God. Think of Jesus' tears and all the implications of the verse "Jesus wept." Re-read the section *Is Suffering Punishment for Sin?* and also Wilfred and Debi's testimonies in Chapter 6 of your *Triumph Over Suffering* book. Do you agree with Wilfred and Debi, that God has simply been getting your attention? What did it take for God to get *your* attention?

When we repent and return to Him, it does not necessarily mean that suffering will be removed. We may live with the consequences of our sins for our entire lives. Why do you think God may not remove the consequences?

Day Four: Look up Job 42:6. If Job is **blameless and upright** (2:3), why did he feel a need to repent? We are going to take a tour of Job and see if we can find an answer to that question. Read Job 1:22 (after he has lost all his possessions and children) and 2:10b (after he has lost his health). What is the difference in these two verses? Do you think it is significant?

Read the following passages from Job and then answer the questions:
    Job 10:1, 13:3, 27:6, 32:1, 33:17-28, 38:1-6, 40:1-2,8, 42:1-6

How would you categorize Job's sin?

This is shocking. Upright and blameless Job was in sin . . . what about us?

   Why did God allow Satan to attack Job? Was it merely to teach the heavenlies, or was there even more going on? Did God allow Satan to "sift him like wheat?" Job 32:1 tells us Job was righteous in his own eyes. Could it be that God was decreeing suffering for Job to discipline him and to expose his sin?

   Read one last passage, Job 42:10-17. God gave Job sheep, camels, oxen, donkeys, and children. But . . . what about Job's health? Does it say? Do you think it is implied that God restored his health? If you think God did not restore his health, why do you think God did not?

   Realize blameless and upright does not mean sinless. Through his suffering, God revealed to Job his pride in his self-righteousness. When his eyes were opened to his sin and he repented, God grew him in righteousness and integrity.

Day Five: Why does God desire to expose our sin? Read 1 Peter 4:1-2. What happens when we suffer in the flesh, in the body?

Read 2 Peter 1:3-4. Stunning! God wants us to be partakers of His divine nature, to share His divine nature! Can you even comprehend that He would offer us this? What happens when we participate in His divine nature?

Read 2 Peter 1:5-11. Do you possess these qualities in an increasing manner? Spend some time now alone with the Lord, meditating on where you stand with each of these eight qualities. Journal what He shows you.

If you possess these qualities in increasing measure, you will not be ineffective or unproductive, useless or unfruitful. These are piercing words. Remember it is the kindness of God that leads us to repentance (Rom 2:4). Journal your thoughts.

Day Six: We want so desperately to partake in His divine nature. Why doesn't God conform us to Christ's image overnight? Read Matthew 12:43-45.

How could the evil spirits get back in? If the house is swept clean, why would the evil spirits even want to go back in? Read an Old Testament parallel, Exodus 23:27-30, which describes how the Israelites will take possession of the Promised Land. Why are they not allowed to eliminate their enemies all at once?

Why do you think the wild animals would be able to become too numerous?

It is possible the wild animals are also symbolic, referring to the state of anarchy that often appears when there is not a strong government in place. Relate this Exodus passage to Jesus' parable. If a man's sins are revealed to him all at once, and he sweeps his house clean and puts it in order but leaves his house_____, wild animals, anarchy, greater sins can overrun it.

Who should fill our house when darkness is swept out? _____

The Israelites would be allowed to take further possession of the land when they increased enough or became fruitful enough. We must grow spiritually, so we are prepared to receive more of the Holy Spirit's power. The greater the suffering, the greater the growth potential. When we grow spiritually through these tremendous trials, when we triumph over suffering, God will infuse His Spirit into us more. Relate this to the Spirit occupying your heart.

Day Seven: We are going to take suffering to the next level: suffering unjustly. Read 1 Peter 2:19-25. Write verse 21 below:

We are called to suffer unjustly, just as our King suffered unjustly. Jesus suffered unjustly, and as a result of that unjust suffering, reconciled men to God. How does this change your perception of unjust suffering you or others you know have experienced?

If we are suffering because of our own sins, and we repent and turn to Him, He may or may not remove the suffering. Either way, will He *still* use this suffering for our good and for His Kingdom? Absolutely. However, suffering unjustly is simply suffering on a whole new level. Journal your thoughts.

We are halfway through this course! Persevere, for the treasure of a changed heart is more valuable than a precious jewel.

Chapter 7
Suffering Can Teach Us Humility, Dependence, and Forgiveness

Scripture Verses for the Week:

"When I fed them, they were satisfied; when they were satisfied, they became proud; then they forgot me."

Hosea 13:6

Day One: Read Chapter 7, Suffering Can Teach Us Humility, Dependence, and Forgiveness, in your *Triumph Over Suffering* book. You may want to spend more time in the sections that are most relevant to you right now.

Which verse speaks to your heart? Write down that verse, and journal your thoughts.

Day Two:

He delivers the afflicted in their affliction, and opens their ear in time of oppression.

Job 36:15 NASB

God has so much to say when we are suffering. Since our routines and busy lives are now interrupted, God can capture our attention. Independence, pride, and unforgiveness are three areas He may address. If we are open, He will reveal to us that our superficial humility was really not much humility at all, that what we thought was complete dependence was dependence in only one corner of our lives, and that forgiveness comes in many layers.

Write down these verses, circling any words that have struck you.

Galatians 6:3

Philippians 2:3

Proverbs 26:12

Listen to what God is telling you, and write down what you have heard.

How might God test us to reveal our pride to us? Read Proverbs 27:21 to find out. Then journal a time when you were tested in this way.

Day Three: Read a shocking passage about a prideful man in Daniel 4:1-37. Write down verse 37b, and how you can apply this message to your life.

John the Baptist says of Jesus, **"He must increase, but I must decrease."** (Jn 3:30 NASB). What does John mean by this? How can you apply it to your life?

Day Four: Let's explore dependence. Read John 15:1-8. Remain or abide in the Greek is meno, literally "to stay ... dwell, remain, stand" - and my favorite, "to tarry."[1] Figuratively meno means "to be and remain united with him, one with him in heart, mind, and will."[2] How do we dwell in Him? Tarry with Him? How will dwelling in Him lead to being united with Him in heart, mind, and will?

"Apart from me you can do nothing."   John 15:5
  Nothing literally means *nothing*. Apply that to your life right now.

  It's your turn to illustrate Scripture! Use this page to create a visual image for these verses from John 15. Realize that the "vine" of a grape vine is not a skinny branch; it is a *thick* trunk. Do not be intimidated – stick figures are fine. You can use colored pencils, markers, pencil, pen, whatever you choose. Do not skip this assignment. The picture you create will sear an image of dependence into your mind like nothing else can.

---

[1] James Strong, *The New Strong's Exhaustive Concordance of the Bible, Concise Dictionary of the Words in the Greek, Testament,* p 56 (no. 3306).
[2] Zodhiates, p 960.

Day Five: No one wants to be wheelchair-bound, dependent on others to dress them, feed them, take them places. No one wants to be poor, dependent on others for food and shelter. No one wants to be dependent upon others for money, childcare, even help with ministry work. We naturally want to do it on our own.

The more gifted we are, the further away from complete dependence upon God we may be. God may put us in a position of physical dependence because that enables us to come closer to the total physical, emotional, and spiritual dependence He desires for us. The more dependent we are upon Him, the more He releases His Spirit to work in us.

When God has placed us in a place of dependence and calls us to Kingdom work, all who see will know that it was not our work, but God's. If others see us as independent strong people, sadly, when God works through us, others will see *us* and not God. What does the verse below mean to you?

For you have died, and your life is hidden with Christ in God.
Colossians 3:3

It is the cry of our hearts: for our lives to be hidden with Christ in God. For people to **see our good works**, and instead of glorifying us, to **praise your Father in heaven** (Mt 5:16). When we are in an obvious state of dependence, we will not have this struggle. Do you have a thorn in your flesh, or a hip wrenched from your socket, that is teaching you complete dependence? Does this illuminate a more vivid understanding of suffering for you?

Day Six: We are going to read some of Jesus' words on forgiveness in the Lord's Prayer, but before you turn to that passage, understand that these verses are not describing salvation. Salvation is a free gift, by grace through faith (Eph 2:8). We cannot earn God's forgiveness by forgiving. God mercifully offers His forgiveness freely to all; we can choose to accept it or reject it. We accept God's forgiveness and His offer of salvation when we accept Jesus as our Savior.

Remember who was asking Jesus, **"Teach us to pray."** Jesus' teachings here are directed to Christians, His disciples, those who have already accepted God's forgiveness, those who can call God their Father. Read Matthew 6:12, 14-15 and write these verses below.

Now read Matthew 18: 21-35. This is a sobering parable, many would say quite disturbing. To imagine God **turning him over to the jailers to be tortured** simply does not sit right with us. It does not even seem in character with God. What do you think?

Let's take another angle. When we live in unforgiveness, guess who suffers the most? The person who is unforgiven? Usually not. Generally, the one who suffers most is the one who is refusing to forgive. The unforgiven one often doesn't even know they are unforgiven, or if they do know, they don't even care. So the one who is refusing to forgive is living in a torturous place of their own creation, allowing unforgiveness to torment them, to eat away at their heart and soul. When we choose unforgiveness, we choose to torture ourselves; we create our own prison; our unforgiveness is our jailer. This may be God simply turning us over to the natural consequences of unforgiveness. Disciplining us for our good. What do you think?

Sometimes, we may be living in unforgiveness and not even recognize it. Be still before the Lord. Let Him reveal to your heart anyone you are not forgiving.

What will you do now?

Day Seven: Study what forgiveness is and what it is not in the section *Exchanging Unforgiveness for Forgiveness* in Chapter 7 of your *Triumph Over Suffering* book. If you have identified someone you have not forgiven, fill in the chart below.

The pain or hurt you are accepting	
How it is significant	
Why it really does matter	
Your commitment to refuse to take the blame	
How you will resist the urge to twist things around to be your fault	
How you will deny their request to excuse them	
If you are inclined to pity them, how you will handle it	
What it will take for them to earn your trust again	
Your choice to release the wrongdoer from your bitterness and vengeance	

Look up 2 Corinthians 2:7-11. This is petrifying – Satan uses unforgiveness to outwit us, to take advantage of us, for we are inviting him into our lives. Do not give him a foothold; do not be ignorant of his schemes. Journal your thoughts.

If you have chosen humility, dependence, forgiveness, Jesus has released you from your chains and lifted that burden from you! Hallelujah!

Chapter 8
Spiritual Warfare:
Suffering To Advance the Kingdom

Scripture Verses for the Week:

For our struggle is not against flesh and blood, but against the rulers, against the authorities, against the powers of this dark world and against the spiritual forces of evil in the heavenly realms. Therefore put on the full armor of God . . .

Ephesians 6:12-13

Day One: Of all the chapters in this book, Satan does not want you to work through this one. Do not forget to pray first, then read Chapter 8, Spiritual Warfare: Suffering To Advance the Kingdom, in your *Triumph Over Suffering* book.

Which verse speaks to your heart? Write down that verse, and journal your thoughts.

Day Two: Look up the following verses and answer the questions.

2 Chronicles 16:9
    Do you desire to be the one the Lord's eyes rest upon as He searches the earth for a heart fully committed to Him? What if that means suffering? Do you still want your heart to be completely His?

2 Timothy 4:6
    A drink offering of Old Testament times was completely poured out upon the altar of sacrifice. Are you pouring yourself out like a drink offering? What exactly does that mean to you?

Luke 9:62
    Fit literally means "well-situated ... useful."[1] If we are not fully committed to Him, if we are not ready to make whatever changes are necessary in our life to follow His call, we are simply not useful to Him. That is gut-wrenching.
    Have you ever had a time in your walk with Christ that you put your hand to the plow and *looked back*? What happened? How did you feel? What brought you back to the plow? Was it too late to resume the work?

---

[1] Zodhiates, p 673 (no. 2111).

Chapter 8 ~ Spiritual Warfare: Suffering To Advance the Kingdom

Day Three: Read Rev 3:15-16. What do you think hot, lukewarm, and cold mean?

Time for a spiritual checkup. Pray, and fill in the chart below. Place yourself in the cold, lukewarm, or hot categories, and write why you would place yourself there.

	Cold	Lukewarm	Hot
Bible reading			
Church attendance			
Prayer			
Hearing God's voice			
Others know you are Christian			
Convicted of sins and repenting			
Growing in Christ			
Ministry Work			
Heart Broken for Unsaved			
Sharing the Gospel			
Life has significant purpose for God			
Priorities are God's priorities			
Abiding in Christ			
Fellowship and accountability			
Living to glorify God			
Add a category:			

As you evaluate your heart through this check up, would God call you cold, lukewarm, or hot? Circle the thermometer that best characterizes your spiritual state right now, and explain why in the space below the thermometers.

Is this the category you want to be in? Will you do anything differently?

The literal translation of the word spit is "vomit."[1] Why do you think Jesus is vomiting out the lukewarm ones? Why not the cold ones?

---

[1] Zodhiates, p 574 (no. 1692).

Day Four: Describe a time when you recognized His Kingdom was advanced. Was suffering involved?

Go over the verses in Chapter 8 in your *Triumph Over Suffering* book in the section entitled *Is Suffering Inevitable for Christians?*

What do you think? Is suffering inevitable? Ordained? Planned? Do you think suffering is necessary to advance His Kingdom? Why or why not?

Before answering the next question, be sure you know what spiritual warfare is, and what it is not. Turn to Chapter 8 in your *Triumph Over Suffering* book and review the section entitled *Suffering is Your Divine Appointment*.

Ask the Lord to open your eyes to see what He sees. Is spiritual warfare causing your suffering? Does this give you a more vivid understanding of your tribulations?

Day Five: In Chapter 8 of your *Triumph Over Suffering* book in the section *Spiritual Weapons,* read what Peter learned from his time of sifting, 1 Peter 5:5-10.

When we are attacked, if we choose the spiritual weapons of humility, casting anxiety on Him, and being alert, the Holy Spirit will enable us to resist Satan and stand firm. To resist Satan is to refuse to succumb to his temptations. To stand firm is to cling to God in full surrender and obedience, no matter how great the suffering is; to hold that crucial position in battle.

There will be a four-fold result of that victory (verse 10 NIV): God will Himself

_____ you & make you _____, _____, and _____.

- restore = katartizo = "to put a thing in its appropriate condition"[1]
- make you strong = sthenoo = "to strengthen"[2]
- firm = sterizo = "to set fast"[3] the way Jesus "steadfastly set His face to go to Jerusalem" (Lk 9:51 KJV)
- steadfast = themelioo = "to lay the foundation"[4]

Spectacular. Peter tells us when the roaring lion attacks us, we are to humble ourselves. We are not think of ourselves more highly than we ought (Rom 12:3), but admit the truth about our unworthiness and powerlessness. If we then run to God, casting our anxiety upon Him, God will lift us up in His time. If we resist Satan and do not succumb to his temptations, if we cling to Jesus and remain surrendered and obedient, God will use this suffering to mold us into the person He desires us to be. He will strengthen us physically and spiritually and turn us resolutely in the direction He is calling us. He will lay in us the rock solid foundation of Jesus, a foundation to build our faith upon. If you have been through spiritual warfare, journal your experiences of this most amazing result. Or, if you are in the midst of spiritual warfare, write a prayer asking Him to use this trial to restore you and make you strong, firm, and steadfast.

---

[1] Zodhiates, p 842 (no. 2675).
[2] Zodhiates, p-1287 (no. 4599).
[3] Zodhiates, p 1313 (no 4741).
[4] Zodhiates, p 729 (no. 2311).

Day Six: In Chapter 8 of your *Triumph Over Suffering* book in the section *Spiritual Weapons,* read the passage from 2 Corinthians that describes spiritual weapons. With these spiritual weapons from 2 Corinthians and 1 Peter fresh in your mind, fill in the chart below. There are no right or wrong answers; this is just an exercise to help you recognize spiritual warfare and to choose a divinely powerful spiritual weapon instead of a weapon of the flesh.

Satan's Attack	**Do Not Use** this weapon of the flesh	**Do Use** this divinely powerful spiritual weapon
Financial problems	Worry	
Disrupting a relationship	Justify yourself and perpetuate argument	
Doubt	Try to prove yourself to Satan or to the world	
Tempt you to sin	Make excuses – "It's not so bad a sin" – and succumb to the temptation	
Suck the life out of you spiritually	Think you can do this on your own strength	
Illness, injury, or suffering	Become obsessed with relief of the suffering or with physical healing	
Lead you into a trap	Become smug, sure you will not fall into that trap	
Accuse you of sin	Defend yourself, or deny your sin	
Add your own attack:		

Day Seven: Read 2 Kings 6:8-23 (**man of God** in verse 9 is the prophet Elisha).
The warfare that is going on in the heavens is more real than our physical world – yet we are mostly unaware of it. When the spiritual eyes of Elisha's servant were opened, he was able to see the mighty army of God's Angels of Light arrayed for battle. Read again verse 16:

"Don't be _____," the prophet answered. "Those who are with us are _____ _____ those who are with them."   2 Kings 6:16

There is much more to this passage. Read again verses 22-23. Amazing, how Elisha instructed the King of Israel to treat his enemies, and the end result. This is parallel to our instructions in the New Testament. Read the verses below, and summarize how we are called to treat those who hurt us:
   Luke 6:27-38   Romans 12:20-21   1 Peter 3:9   Proverbs 24:17-18

Why do you think God commands us to treat those who hurt us in this way?

People are not our enemies. Family, friends, other Christians, even those who do not belong to Christ are not our enemies. Satan wants you to fall into the trap of fighting with weapons of the flesh. If your relationships are in turmoil, recognize that the warfare is spiritual, and overcome evil with good. Using all you have learned this week, determine how you will handle those relationships differently now.

Go back to page 29 in this Workbook. *Now that you have completed Part II, Absolute Sovereignty, where would you place yourself on the graph? Draw in a new figure. Behold, God has conformed you more closely to the image of Christ!*

Part III:
Intimacy With Christ
Seize Your Purpose Through Your Suffering

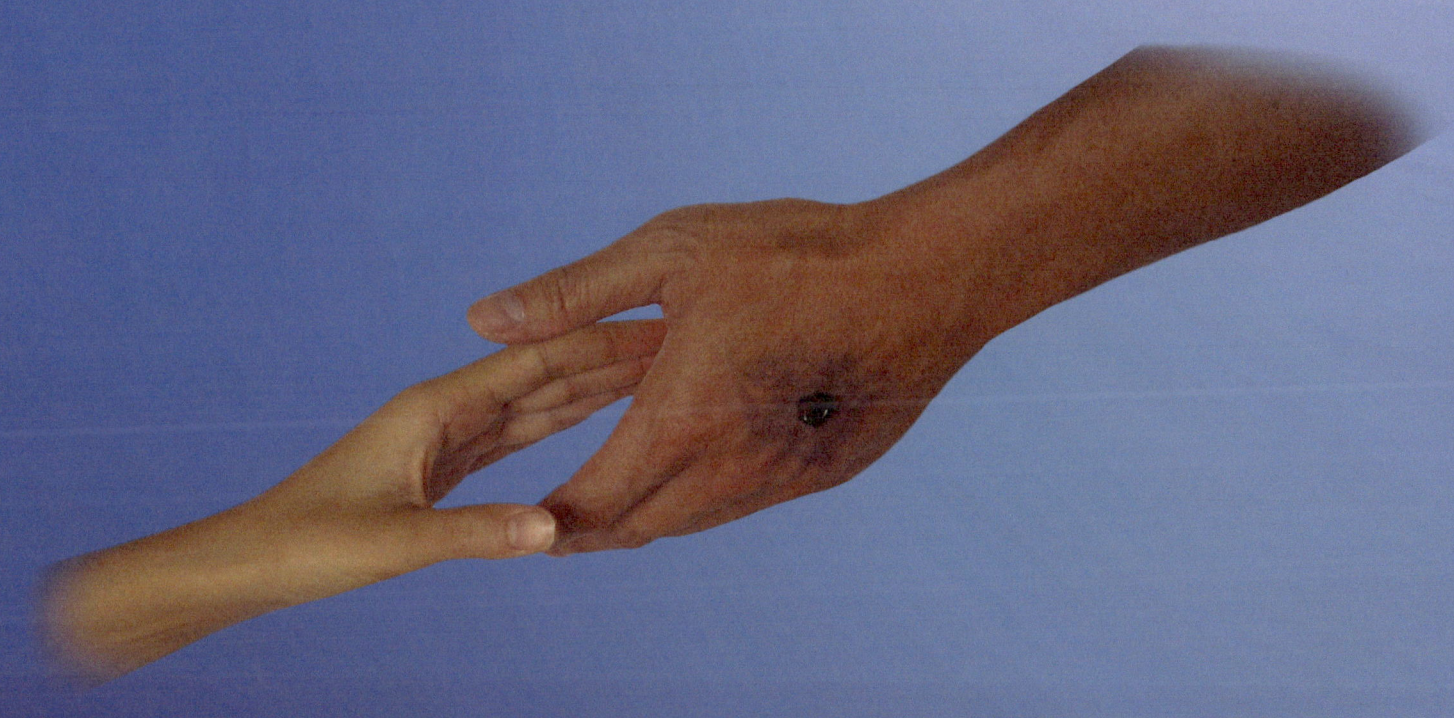

9 *Suffering Can Lead To Intimacy With Christ*	66
10 *How Will You Respond To Your Suffering?*	74
11 & 12 *Hearing the Voice of God & Seize What Jesus Seized You For*	81

Chapter 9
Suffering Can Lead To Intimacy With Christ

Scripture Verses for the Week:

> I consider everything a loss compared to the surpassing greatness of knowing Christ Jesus my Lord, for whose sake I have lost all things. I consider them rubbish, that I may gain Christ and be found in him . . . I want to know Christ and the power of his resurrection and the fellowship of sharing in his sufferings, becoming like him in his death . . .
>
> Philippians 3:8-10

Day One: Read Chapter 9, Suffering Can Lead To Intimacy With Christ, in your *Triumph Over Suffering* book. When your suffering seems truly meaningless, this is the chapter you will want to know in great depth.

Which verse speaks to your heart? Write down that verse, and journal your thoughts.

Day Two: What do you think of Jesus, in His resurrected body, still bearing the scars of His crucifixion?

When we are suffering, we may wonder, can Jesus relate? Pause a moment and ponder what we know about Jesus' life on earth:

Poverty? To the extreme.
Oppression? He lived in a land that Rome ruled with an iron fist.
Physical pain? Excruciating.
Abandonment? By all His trusted friends, on the night He needed them the most.
Spiritual devastation? Hear His words when He took the weight of the sins of the world onto Himself, **"My God, my God, why have you forsaken me?"** (Mt 27:46)

We studied thlipsis, tribulation, in the *Triumph Over Suffering* book. Jesus understands suffering that is so great it is as if you are an olive crushed with a millstone until the oil drips out. *Jesus* can relate to *you*. The real question is, can *you* relate to *Him*? When you meet Him in heaven, what scars will speak of your passionate love for Him?

Day Three:
"He who eats My flesh and drinks My blood abides in Me, and I in him."
John 6:56 NASB

Have you ever used that phrase? "I eat, drink, and breathe football," or "I exist for thrills," or "I live for my job" – or whatever your passion is. **Abide** is to eat and drink Jesus. Go back to page 52 of this *Workbook* to see abide (meno) again.

Look up Hebrews 12:29. What do you think this verse means?

Look up Exodus 34:14. What a remarkable Name of God: Jealous. The Hebrew is Qanna. Qanna does not mean that God is suspicious, distrustful, or envious. Qanna means that He "will not tolerate the worship of other gods. This word is always used to describe God's attitude toward the worship of false gods, which arouses His jealousy and anger in judgment against the idol worshipers."[1]

When we do not give God our exclusive devotion, when something or someone is above God in our life, we are worshiping an idol. God wants to be in relationship with us. Yes, we were created for His pleasure – but He also created us *to love us*. Since *He* created us, only *He* truly knows what is best for us, what will give us pleasure. Somehow, our complete devotion to Him, our exclusive adoration of our Creator, opens the floodgates to His amazing love. When we are not wholly committed to Him, when we worship idols, when we place other things in our lives above Him, we erect a barrier and are unable to receive that flood of love. His Name is Jealous, Qanna – for *our* good, not for His.

Have you come to know Him most in the deepest of suffering? Has your suffering brought you to the end of your rope, demolished all your idols, as you realized the world has nothing to offer you? Would you ever have come to this point of complete trust in Him without the suffering? Have you encountered Him as Qanna, and almost drowned in the sea of His love, recognizing that He so desires to be your everything?

---

[1] Baker, p 1000 (no. 7067).

Day Four: Turn to Psalm 57 to read about the purest form of worship, worship in suffering. When David wrote this psalm, he had been anointed King years ago, but God had not yet set him on the throne. He was running for his life from Saul. Read and pray through this psalm.

Do you worship God with the fervor of this psalm when you are looking death in the face? When life is not turning out as you had planned? When your suffering involves unbearable pain, or emotional turmoil beyond words? When you thought God gave you a calling, but your work was thwarted with suffering – for years? Would God call you a man or a woman "after My own heart" (1Sa 13:14)?

Read Acts 16:22-34. What do you think of Paul and Silas' midnight song? If you are suffering right now, it is "midnight" for you. Can you sing a song of praise to Him? Can you worship Him with the purest form of worship? Write your song of praise to Him below.

But thou art holy, O thou that inhabitest the praises of Israel.
Psalm 22:3 KJV

God inhabits our praise. When we worship purely, God shows up. What happened in the prison (Acts 16:26)?

And what was the final result of Paul and Silas' pure worship (Acts 16:34)?

I would sure call that advancement of the Kingdom through suffering! Memorize a Scripture verse of praise that you will use when you are in the throes of agony. (You may consider 1 Timothy 6:15-16 or Romans 11:33-36.) Write it here, and write your commitment to praise Him when in the midst of adversity.

Chapter 9 ~ *Suffering To Know Jesus Intimately*

Day Five: Read 1 Corinthians 12:12-27. Then write verse 26 here:

Review the section entitled *Suffering for the Church* in Chapter 9 of your *Triumph Over Suffering* book.

This is an extraordinary idea: intimacy with Jesus translating to intimacy with the church. As we grow more intimate with Christ, we become willing to suffer for the church and even die for the church. Do not think of the church as a building, or even as the people in your home church. Understand the church as everyone who belongs to Jesus. Think of being willing to suffer and die for any of them. Think of being willing to suffer and die for the unsaved, for those who have not yet given their lives to Christ, but will become members of His family, His church, in upcoming days.

Re-read Kim and Joe's stories in this chapter. Kim suffered for her daughter's spiritual growth. Joe went through hip surgery for that old orthopedic surgeon to be saved and his huddle group to explode in their evangelism efforts. Have you reached that level of intimacy with Christ yet? Are you willing to write a commitment of your willingness to suffer in whatever way He decrees in order that His Kingdom be advanced?

Day Six: Read Psalm 90:4 and 2 Peter 3:8. What does earthly time mean to God?

Read Ecclesiastes 3:1-8.

The concept of seasons can be a difficult one to embrace. Yet if we do not recognize that God works through our lives in a seasonal fashion, we may find ourselves fighting against the trials of a particular season, instead of allowing Him to work through those trials to grow us. We may find ourselves impatient for the trial to end, instead of recognizing that God is simply not bound by earthly space and time; the trial will be over when He has accomplished His purposes. What season are you in now?

Do you come to know Him most when you are in the deepest of suffering? Do you develop a closeness that can only result from complete dependence on Him? Or, if you cannot find Him in your suffering, do you treasure the fierce searching because it brings out the intensity of your desire for Him in a way that does not happen when life is smooth? When you are in the season of suffering, do you want out, only to want back in during the season of rest because you are desperate for that closeness?

Day Seven: Go over Philippians 3:8-10, your memory verse for the week.

Joni Eareckson Tada, who has been wheelchair-bound since she was a teenager, writes, "I would rather be in this chair knowing him, than on my feet without him."[1] I have left room for you to write.

Someday, when we are with our Savior in eternity, we will surely consider it all rubbish. It is my prayer for you that you will consider it all rubbish right now, in view of your passionate closeness to Him.

---

[1] Joni Eareckson Tada, *When God Weeps*, Grand Rapids, MI, Zondervan, 1997, p 181.

Chapter 10
How Will You Respond To Your Suffering?

Scripture Verses for the Week:

. . . one thing I do: forgetting what lies behind and reaching forward to what lies ahead, I press on toward the goal for the prize of the upward call of God in Christ Jesus.

Philippians 3:13-14 NASB

Day One: Read Chapter 10, How Will You Respond To Your Suffering? in your *Triumph Over Suffering* book. You may find it full of surprises.

Which verse speaks to your heart? Write down that verse, and journal your thoughts.

Day Two: Refer to the section *Turning Away From God In Suffering* in Chapter 10 in your *Triumph Over Suffering* book. Do the responses of bitterness, hedonism, busyness, or squelching emotions and desires apply to you?

As you analyze the fifth response, praying for relief of suffering, realize that we are certainly to ask, but are to be sure we are asking in complete humility, our hearts bowed to His perfect will and plan. Explain, in your own words, how praying for relief of suffering can become an obsession and drive you away from God. Then examine the methods and motives in your heart when you are asking.

When we are obsessed with the lifting of the suffering, obsessed with having our prayers answered how *we* think they should be answered, we are simply selfish. We want what we think is "best" for ourselves; we are not putting others first; we are not focusing on glorifying God. When we concentrate on relief of the suffering, we miss the plan He has for us *in* the suffering. Read John 13:1-17, and write verse 14 in the space below. Spend some time quiet and humble before God, asking Him to reveal to you any selfishness in your heart.

Day Three: When Jesus was dying, He cried out, **"My God, my God, why have you forsaken me?"** (Mk 15:34). This is the first verse of Psalm 22. In Jesus' time, speaking the first verse of a psalm indicated you were praying the entire psalm. Read through this psalm, and think of Jesus praying these words on the cross.

Note that only the first two verses are questioning God's faithfulness. Verse 3 moves right into praise, and most of this psalm is a prayer of praise to God. When we praise Him, we set Him on the throne of our heart, we tell Him we submit to Him.

What word is repeated three times in verses 4 and 5? _____
Why is that key when we are suffering?

Read verses 6-8 and 12-18. God wants to hear about the intensity of our trial from *our* viewpoint! We know He will weep with us, He will never mock us or ridicule us, He will only treat us with the most tender love. What are your thoughts?

Compare verse 8 with Matthew 27:43, and verse 18 with John 19:24. Now read closely verse 16 of Psalm 22. Realize this psalm was written about a thousand years before crucifixion was invented.

Note how verses 19-21 stand in stark contrast to verses 1 and 2. How did Jesus move from the despair of verses 1 and 2 to the hope of verses 19-21? (Hint: Read the KJV translation of verse 3 on page 70 of this *Workbook*.)

The word **afflicted** in verse 24 and **poor** in verse 26 (NASB **afflicted**) is anav which encompasses being "in a state of oppression" yet also "to bow down, to humble oneself."[1] When we are in the midst of adversity and we remain humble, He does not despise our suffering. He hears our cry for help, and He feeds us. Will He feed us with food, or something else? (Hint: see Jn 6:35).

Summarize the response to suffering that pleases God that you have learned from the One who never sinned.

---
[1] Baker, p 852. (no. 6031).

Chapter 10 ~ How Will You Respond To Your Suffering? 77

Day Four: From *The Response That Pleases God* in Chapter 10 of your *Triumph Over Suffering* book, write the three elements of the response that glorifies God: _____, _____, _____.

Read about traps in Chapter 10 in your *Triumph Over Suffering* book in the section *Adversity is Satan's Trap*. What kinds of trials, situations, and attitudes do you realize are a trap for you, keeping you from the response that glorifies God? How will you successfully avoid these traps?

Read Matthew 13:20-21. "Falls away" is the same word, trap. What does this verse teach you about avoiding Satan's traps? How will you be sure your roots are deep?

Face forward. Paul often uses the analogy of a race to emphasize this aspect of our response. Read Acts 20:24 and 1 Corinthians 9:24-27. What does Paul mean by finishing the course? What course are you running? Are you in strict training? Are you running aimlessly, or are you running to win the prize?

Day Five: Learn contentment. Emphasis is on "learn," a gradual process.

Prayer of an Unknown Confederate Soldier

I asked for strength that I might achieve;
> I was made weak that I might learn humbly to obey.

I asked for health that I might do greater things;
> I was given infirmity that I might do better things.

I asked for riches that I might be happy;
> I was given poverty that I might be wise.

I asked for power that I might have the praise of men;
> I was given weakness that I might feel the need of God.

I asked for all things that I might enjoy life;
> I was given life that I might enjoy all things.

I got nothing that I asked for, but everything that I had hoped for;
> Almost, despite myself, my unspoken prayers were answered;
> I am among men, most richly blessed.[1]

Re-read the definition of makarios, blessed, from the section *Second Key: Learn Contentment* in Chapter 10 of your *Triumph Over Suffering* book. Do you think the soldier's prayer was answered? What have you asked for? What have you been given? Were your prayers answered? Are you content?

I have heard it said that God only gives three possible answers to our requests:
> "Yes." ~ "Not yet." ~ "I have something better!"

What do you think?

Makarios implies favored. I have heard Beth Moore put it this way: "Not that God loves the suffering ones more, but that we have more of His attention for the moment." Because the Lord is not relieving our suffering, He is giving us His precious attention. Bask in it.

---

[1] John Ellis Large, *Think On These Things*, NY, NY, Harper and Brothers Publishers, 1997, p 104.

Day Six: **Rejoice.** In Chapter 10 of your *Triumph Over Suffering* book, in the section entitled *Third Key: Rejoice,* go over the list of reasons to rejoice.

There are some things we can learn from Scripture reading, praying, and serving. However, for many of these blessings, suffering is the *only* way to learn them! From this Why Rejoice? list, what have you taken to heart? What is still fuzzy in your understanding?

I trust you have a good handle on the Why Rejoice? list. Yet what if . . .
    . . . Our suffering was *solely* to display God's glory?
    . . . And what if that means a thorn?
    . . . And what if we were never to understand *why* while on this earth?

Would you still rejoice? That is the ultimate challenge to which God calls us. Look up Psalm 126:5 and apply it to your life.

Day Seven:

Therefore do not be ashamed of the testimony of our Lord or of me His prisoner, but join with me in suffering for the gospel according to the power of God . . . No soldier in active service entangles himself in the affairs of everyday life, so that he may please the one who enlisted him as a soldier . . . Remember Jesus Christ, risen from the dead, descendant of David, according to my gospel, for which I suffer hardship even to imprisonment as a criminal; but the word of God is not imprisoned. For this reason I endure all things for the sake of those who are chosen, so that they also may obtain the salvation which is in Christ Jesus and with it eternal glory.

2 Timothy 1:8, 2:4, 2:8-10 NASB

Do not lose sight of the fact that we are soldiers in a cosmic battle. We are here to please our Commanding Officer, and we must guard ourselves so as not to become entangled in everyday life. We must expect warfare, hardship, and suffering for the sake of the unsaved, for the sake of the gospel, for the sake of those He is calling to His eternal glory.

God is calling . . . are you entangled in everyday life? Or are you able and willing to respond, **"Here I am. Send me!"** (Is 6:8)?

Remarkable, how far God has taken you through this course. From pain and anger to peace and acceptance. From asking "Why me?" to facing forward, learning contentment, and rejoicing. What a metamorphoo!

Chapters 11 and 12
Hearing the Voice of God
and
Seize What Jesus Seized You For

Scripture Verse for the Week:

"What I tell you in the dark, speak in the daylight; what is whispered in your ear, proclaim from the roofs."

Matthew 10:27

Day One: This week, as we tackle the final two chapters, the growth you experienced through this course will explode into an understanding of God's purpose for your life. Today, read Chapter 11, Hearing the Voice of God, in your *Triumph Over Suffering* book.

Which verse speaks to your heart? Write down that verse, and journal your thoughts.

Day Two: We all want to hear God from the burning bush: **"Moses! Moses!.. Take off your sandals, for the place where you are standing is holy ground."** (Ex 3:4-5). Or when we are lying in our beds at night: **"Samuel! Samuel!"** (1Sa 3:10). Or through a vision, like Paul, of the man from Macedonia calling, **"Come over to here and help us."** (Acts 16:9). Yet the truth is that the most common ways God speaks to us are through _____ and _____.

Of course He will speak through Scripture – it is His *Word*! Sometimes I think God does not answer us right away because He wants us to keep coming back to Him. His timing may not be to our liking, but it is always His perfect timing. How often do you hear His voice?

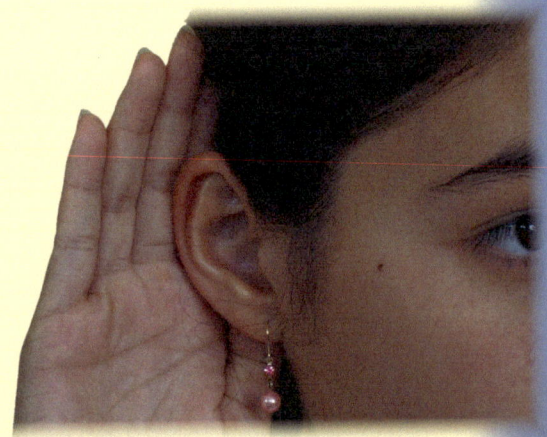

The Lord confides in those who fear him; he makes his covenant known to them.
                                Psalm 25:14

Give yourself a spiritual checkup. List the four keys from the section entitled *Developing an Open Heart* in Chapter 11 of your *Triumph Over Suffering* book.

1-

2-

3-

4-

What did you learn? What will you do differently?

Day Three: Today we will talk about a time God may withdraw from us. Read 2 Chronicles 32:1-31. (You can read about the "sign" referred to in this passage in Isaiah 38:1-8.) Pay special attention to 2 Chronicles 32:25 and 31. What did you learn?

When we have sinned and repent, God may test us to see if it is a true repentance. Hezekiah was at first proud and not thankful (v 25); he then humbled the pride of his heart. Next God tested him and **left him alone** (v 31). Have you experienced this? How did you handle it?

Read 2 Kings 18:1-7 for a summary of Hezekiah's life. Do you think he passed the test?

Day Four: What does God's voice sound like? Sometimes He thunders. His voice booms, breaks cedars, flashes lightning, twists oaks and strips forests bare. Read Psalm 29:3-11. (Realize that when you hear Him thunder, it may not be audible, but powerfully loud in your heart.) Have you heard God in this way?

Yet, sometimes, perhaps more often, He whispers. Carefully read 1 Kings 19:11-13. In this passage, God's voice is translated gentle whisper (NIV and NLT), gentle blowing (NASB), or still small voice (KJV). Have you heard God in this way?

What do you learn about God by reading these two passages?

Which way does He speak to you more often? What will you do in order to keep His still small voice from being overwhelmed by the noises of the world?

Day Five: I described God's calling on your life in Chapter 11 as often vague at first, like an object seen way off in the distance. Over time it will take definite shape as you obey what you understand and God then brings it into focus a bit more. Why do you think He does not reveal His entire plan for your life immediately?

Read Genesis 25:21-26 and Genesis 27:1-39. In these passages, God had revealed to Rebekah His plan: Esau would serve Jacob. What did Rebekah do to ensure all would happen according to what God had revealed to her?

Do you think God revealed these things to her so *she* would ensure it happened according to God's plan? Did God need Rebekah to make it happen the way He wanted it to?

Why do you think God often withholds the long-term plan from us? Does this make you more accepting of the way He reveals His calling on our lives?

Days Six and Seven: At the end of Chapter 11, I challenged you to implement this guide to hearing God's voice, praying and fasting to ask God for an understanding deep in your heart of your calling. Have you immersed yourself in prayer?

Read the final chapter, Chapter 12, Seize What Jesus Seized You For, in your *Triumph Over Suffering* book.

God has a calling on your life for which He has equipped you *through* your suffering, a calling that only *you* can fulfill. He has comforted you with His comfort so that you can comfort others. Your suffering is not meaningless! It is for His honor and glory, it is to conform you to the image of Christ, it is to advance His Kingdom, it is to reach the lost for Christ. If God has revealed to you His purpose, journal and e-mail me at CJL@triumphoversuffering.com so I can encourage you and pray for you. If you are listening and waiting, don't give up! Remember how much He desires you to spend time with Him, and e-mail me so I can support you and pray with you.

Beloved in Christ, God is rejoicing over you with singing! You have completed a very daring course, and the Holy Spirit has grown your roots deep. Spend some time alone with Him right now, and allow Him to reveal to you the profound intimacy with which He has blessed you through this course. Well done, good and faithful servant!